A Pageant of Great Women

Cicely Mary Hamilton

Nabu Public Domain Reprints:

You are holding a reproduction of an original work published before 1923 that is in the public domain in the United States of America, and possibly other countries. You may freely copy and distribute this work as no entity (individual or corporate) has a copyright on the body of the work. This book may contain prior copyright references, and library stamps (as most of these works were scanned from library copies). These have been scanned and retained as part of the historical artifact.

This book may have occasional imperfections such as missing or blurred pages, poor pictures, errant marks, etc. that were either part of the original artifact, or were introduced by the scanning process. We believe this work is culturally important, and despite the imperfections, have elected to bring it back into print as part of our continuing commitment to the preservation of printed works worldwide. We appreciate your understanding of the imperfections in the preservation process, and hope you enjoy this valuable book.

Photograph by Miss Leon, 30, Regent Street, S.W. *Copyright.*

Cicely Hamilton.

A Pageant of Great Women

BY

CICELY HAMILTON

Author of "Diana of Dobson's," "Marriage as a Trade," "How the Vote was Won," *etc.*

THE SUFFRAGE SHOP
1910

To
EDITH CRAIG
Whose ideas these lines
were written to illustrate

Forthcoming Publication:
Woman in the New Era.
By Charlotte Despard . . .

This publication is the first issued by The Suffrage Shop, whose promoters intend shortly to open premises in central London for the publication and sale of literature dealing with the Woman's Movement. Until the opening of these premises all orders for books and communications in general should be addressed to The Suffrage Shop, 31, Bedford Street, Strand, W.C.

The Suffrage Shop desires to thank the proprietors of the *Daily Mirror* for permission to use the photographs of Miss Marion Terry as Florence Nightingale, and two groups of the characters; and Miss Lena Connell for that of Miss Ellen Terry as Nance Oldfield.

The Author wishes to acknowledge her indebtedness to Mr. W. H. Margetson, whose Suffrage Cartoon suggested the employment of the figures of Justice, Womanhood and Prejudice.

LIST OF ILLUSTRATIONS

Cicely Hamilton	*Frontispiece*
Maud Hoffman as Madame Roland	Facing page 27
Eva Balfour as Sappho	,, ,, 29
Edith Craig as Rosa Bonheur	,, ,, 29
Ellen Terry as Nance Oldfield	,, ,, 31
Mrs. Despard as St. Hilda	,, ,, 33
Joy Chatwyn as Elizabeth Fry	,, ,, 35
Group of Rulers	,, ,, 37
Suzanne Sheldon as Catherine the Great	,, ,, 39
Vera Coburn as the Maid of Saragossa	,, ,, 41
Cicely Hamilton as Christian Davies	,, ,, 41
Christopher St. John as Hannah Snell	,, ,, 43
Lina Rathbone as Mary Ann Talbot	,, ,, 45
Marion Terry as Florence Nightingale	,, ,, 45
Group of Warriors	,, ,, 47

First produced at the
Scala Theatre, London,
November 10th, 1909

All rights reserved

Assistant Stage Manager: Mr. A. G. Forde
Music arranged by Mr. J. M. Capel

Justice	LADY GROVE
Prejudice	MR. KENYON MUSGROVE
Woman	MISS ADELINE BOURNE

THE LEARNED WOMEN

Hypatia	Miss Elaine Inescourt
St. Teresa	Miss Ada Potter
Lady Jane Grey	Miss Dorothy Finney
Madame de Staël	Miss Frances Vane
Madame Roland	Miss Maude Hoffman
Madame de Scudéry	Miss Nora Royston
Jane Austen	Miss Winifred Mayo
George Sand	Miss Mary Webb
Caroline Herschell	Miss Brineta Browne
Madame Curie	Miss Margaret Marshall
Graduate	Miss Maude Buchanan

THE ARTISTS

Sappho	Miss Eva Balfour
Vittoria Colonna	Miss Gwendoline Bishop
Angelica Kauffmann	Miss Rose Mathews
Vigée le Brun	Miss Margaret Halstan
Rosa Bonheur	Miss Edith Craig
Margaret van Eyck	Miss Irene Ross
Nance Oldfield	Miss Ellen Terry

THE SAINTLY WOMEN

St. Hilda	Miss Madeline Roberts
Elizabeth Fry	Miss Joy Chatwyn
Elizabeth of Hungary	Miss Gwladys Morris
Catherine of Siena	Mrs. Madeline Lucette Ryley

THE HEROIC WOMEN

Charlotte Corday	Mrs. Brown Potter
Flora Macdonald	Miss Mona Harrison
Kate Barlass	Miss Evelyn Hammill
Grace Darling	Miss Barbara Ayrton

THE RULERS

Victoria	Miss Angela Hubbard
Elizabeth	Miss Janette Steer
Zenobia	Miss Nella Powys
Philippa	Mrs. Sam Sothern
Deborah	Miss Edyth Olive
Isabella	Miss Granville
Catherine the Great	Miss Suzanne Sheldon
Tsze-Hsi-An	Miss Viola Finney

THE WARRIORS

Joan of Arc	Miss Pauline Chase
Boadicea	Miss Elizabeth Kirby
Agnes of Dunbar	Miss Frances Wetherall
Emilie Plater	Miss Miriam Lewes
Ranee of Jhansi	Munci Capel
Maid of Saragossa	Miss Vera Coburn
Christian Davies	Miss Cicely Hamilton
Hannah Snell	Miss Christopher St. John
Mary Ann Talbot	Mrs. R. Rathbone
Florence Nightingale	Miss Marion Terry

A PAGEANT OF GREAT WOMEN

JUSTICE (*enthroned.*)

(*To her enters* WOMAN, *pursued by* PREJUDICE. *She kneels at the feet of* JUSTICE.)

JUSTICE.
Why dost thou cling to me? What dost thou ask?

WOMAN.
I cling to Justice and I cry for freedom!

JUSTICE.
Is it not thine already?

WOMAN.
No and no!

JUSTICE.

Art thou not worthy freedom?

WOMAN.

Yea and yea!

PREJUDICE.

Goddess, she speaks but stammering foolishness,
Not knowing what she asks.

WOMAN.

I know and long—

PREJUDICE.

She weeps for that she is not fit to have;
She is a very child in the ways of the world,
A thing protected, covered from its roughness—

WOMAN.

Have I not felt its roughness, suffered and wept?

JUSTICE.

Let him speak on—let him accuse—then answer.

PREJUDICE.

Freedom is born of wisdom—springs from wisdom-
And when was woman wise? Has she not ever
Looked childlike up to man? Has she not ever
Put the outward show before the inward grace?

Scorned learning, lest it dim the light of her eye?
Shunned knowledge, lest long study pale her cheek?
Is not her day a day of petty cares,
Of petty hates and likings?   When has she
Stood godlike in her wisdom, great of soul?
What is her prize in life—a kiss, a smile,
The right to claim caresses!   Yet she cries
For freedom!   An she had it, she would sell it
For a man's arm round her waist!

WOMAN.

Oh, well, indeed, well does this come from you,
Who held the body as all, the spirit as naught—
From you who saw us only as a sex!
Who did your worst and best to quench in us
The very spark and glow of the intellect:
Who blew a jeer at the leap and glimmer of it
And smothered it with laughter! .. This from you
Who praised a simper far above a thought—
Who prized a dimple far beyond a brain!
So were we trained to simper, not to think:
So were we bred for dimples, not for brains!
Not souls, but foolish flesh—so you desired us
And, God have pity, made us! .. Shall you cry
Contempt on your own doing?   Then you cry
Contempt upon yourself!   Had never woman

Photograph by Miss Leon, 30, Regent Street, S.W.   *Copyright.*

Maud Hoffman as Madame Roland.

Been more than roseleaf cheek and pouted lip,
You should be dumb before her meanness—you
Who ask no more of her... Oh, think you well
What you have done to make it hard for her
To dream, to write, to paint, to build, to learn—
Oh, think you well! And wonder at the line
Of those who knew that life was more than love
And fought their way to achievement and to fame!

(THE LEARNED WOMEN *enter.*)

HYPATIA	Hypatia, she whose wisdom brought her death,
	Heads the brave line; and see, the saintly nun,
ST. TERESA	Teresa, guide and leader unto God,
	Writer of living words! Thou ten days queen,
LADY JANE GREY	Poor little maid, the pawn of guiltier minds,
	Thy learning had put many a man to shame!
MADAME DE STAEL	What of the keen De Staël, quick of tongue,
	Polished of pen? Of Manon Roland, what—
MADAME ROLAND	Leader of men, unconquered even in death?
	Boast of romancers—'twas a woman's hand
MLLE. DE SCUDERY	That penned a novel first—de Scudéry's!
	And on her follow her disciples twain,
JANE AUSTEN GEORGE SAND	English Jane Austen and George Sand of France.
	See one who helped to map the stars of heaven—
CAROLINE HERSCHELL	Caroline Herschell! And where is the man

Photograph by Miss Leon, 30, Regent Street, S.W. *Copyright.*

Eva Balfour as Sappho.

Photograph by Miss Leon, 30, Regent Street, S.W. *Copyright.*

Edith Craig as Rosa Bonheur.

	Stands higher in the ranks of science to-day
MADAME CURIE	Than Madame Curie? Last of all the train
	Comes the girl graduate of a modern day,
GRADUATE	Working with man as eagerly and hard—
	And oft enough denied a man's reward.
	And though you barred from us the realms of art—
	Decreeing Love should be our all in all—
	Denying us free thought, free act, free word—
	Yet some there have been burst the silken bonds
	(Harder to burst than steel) and lived and wrought.

(THE ARTISTS *enter.*)

SAPPHO	Thy voice, oh Sappho, down the ages rings!
	Woven of passion and power, thy mighty verse
	Streams o'er the years, a flaming banner of song!
VITTORIA COLONNA	Inspiring others and herself inspired,
	Vittoria Colonna sweeps us by—
ANGELICA KAUFFMANN	Poet and noble dame... Ah, Madame Kauffmann,
	In your day were our painters more gallant,
	Admitting women to due share of honour!
VIGÉE LE BRUN	Vigée le Brun, your sitters live for us
	From far-off years... A man? No—Rosa Bonheur!
ROSA BONHEUR	Back from the horse-fair, virile in her garb
	As virile in her work! Who follows? Sure
	A painter, too, and one of no mean fame—

Photograph by Miss Lena Connell, 50, Grove End Road, N.W.   *Copyright.*

Ellen Terry as Nance Oldfield.

MARGARET VAN EYCK 'Tis that Van Eyck, that Margaret, who shared
A brother's glory!.. Lo, Camargo comes—
CAMARGO A dancer, a dancer, a poem—a song herself!
Lyric of movement, ballad of gliding grace;
Rhythm of lifted hand and poised foot—
Music made manifest!.. Come we last of all
To the living art of the actor—

NANCE OLDFIELD.

NANCE OLDFIELD By your leave,
Nance Oldfield does her talking for herself!
If you, Sir Prejudice, had had your way,
There would be never an actress on the boards.
Some lanky, squeaky boy would play my parts:
And, though I say it, there'd have been a loss!
The stage would be as dull as now 'tis merry—
No Oldfield, Woffington, or—Ellen Terry!

WOMAN.

Have I not answered him?

JUSTICE.

Thou hast answered well!
How sayst thou—art thou still of the same mind?

PREJUDICE.

She is unworthy. In her narrow life,

Photograph by Miss Leon, 30, Regent Street, S.W. *Copyright.*

Mrs. Despard as St. Hilda.

Cramped round and centred in her man, her child,
Is room for no wide love of the outer world—
Is room for no stern duty to her kind.
She only loves the lips that touch her own;
She only serves those who go in and out
At the door of her daily life—being small of heart.

WOMAN.

It is not so!

PREJUDICE.

I cry for proof!

WOMAN.

Shalt have it!

(THE SAINTLY WOMEN *enter.*)

Oh, saintly women, were ye small of heart?

St. Hilda — Thou Mother in God, St. Hilda, answer him!
Abbess and ruler in thy northern home,
Was no wide love of the outer world in thee?

Elizabeth Fry — O, thou dear Friend that wast a friend indeed
To all that sorrowed, being in chains and sin,
Thou sweet Elizabeth, thou saint of the gaol,
Not narrow was the door of thy daily life.

Elizabeth of Hungary — Thou rose-lapped princess, daughter of Hungary,
Thy days were perfumed with a glory of love

Photograph by Miss Leon, 30, Regent Street, S.W. *Copyright.*

Joy Chatwyn as Elizabeth Fry.

And stainless in their pure humility!

ST. CATHERINE OF SIENA — And thou, high Catherine, Siena's child,
Maker of peace 'twixt princes, humbly bred,
Do we not count thee 'mongst the mighty dead?
So pass my saints—not cramped nor mean of soul!
Nor do they pass alone!

(THE HEROINES *enter*.)

      See where they come,
Those who have loved a cause, been loyal to it,
Striven and suffered nobly rather than fail
In a hard duty...
      Look on her who wears

CHARLOTTE CORDAY — The blood-red garb of the condemned—on her
Who took the knife in her small woman's hand,
Who laid the stain of murder on her soul
And met death smiling—steadfast, unashamed!

FLORA MACDONALD — And what of her, the Highland lass, the maid
Whose love unfaltering led a hunted prince,
Whose faith, unbroken, saved a broken man?

KATE BARLASS — Or her, that dauntless Kate, her countrywoman,
Who barred the assassin's pathway with her arm?

GRACE DARLING — And was her deed unworthy of a man—
The frail lone girl who fought through wind and wave,

Photograph by *Daily Mirror.* *Copyright.*
Top row: Viola Finney as Tsze-Hsi-An. Edith Olive as Deborah. Mrs. Sam Sothern as Queen Philippa.
Bottom row: Nella Powys as Zenobia. Janette Steer as Queen Elizabeth. Angela Hubbard as Queen Victoria.

Risking her own, her brethren's life to save?

JUSTICE.

Art answered yet?

PREJUDICE.

Nay, hear me, goddess, hear me!
Give her her freedom, she will strive to rule.
Her brain will reel beneath the sense of power—
She will grow dizzy, grasp at what she knows not!
'Tis man's to reign, 'tis woman's to obey.
The steady outlook, the wide thought are man's.
So Nature has ordained—she cannot rule.

(THE QUEENS *enter*.)

WOMAN.

Queen Elizabeth	Here's Royal Bess to give the lie to him—
	He had not dared to speak it to her face!
Queen Victoria	And see, the little maid of eighteen years
	Who, on a summer morning, woke to find
	Herself a queen, to reign where Bess had reigned.
	You shall not put her, nor shall you put Bess,
	Below the wisest of our line of kings!
Zenobia	Behind, Zenobia of the hero's heart;
Philippa of Hainault	And that Philippa, wise and merciful,
	Who ruled a kingdom for her absent lord

Photograph by Miss Leon, 30, Regent Street, S.W.   Copyright.
Suzanne Sheldon as Catherine the Great.

     And knelt in pity for a humbled foe.
Deborah And thou, O Deborah, judge in Israel,
     Rise up and bear me out! And thou, O Queen,
Isabella of Grave Isabella, prince of proud Castile,
Spain
     Thou who gav'st ear unto a sailor's dream
     To his eternal honour and thine own!
Maria   And when Theresa reigned in Hungary;
Theresa
     And when great Catherine wore the Russian crown;
Catherine II. Who stood more high than they, who ruled more
of Russia
      kingly?
     And was there any in the Flowery Land
Empress of That dared its cunning Empress to outface—
China
Tsze-Hsi-An Born slave, then monarch of a countless race!

PREJUDICE.

All these have ruled because man let them rule,
And not against his will. Come we to that,
Force is the last and ultimate judge: 'tis man
Who laps his body in mail, who takes the sword—
The sword that must decide! Woman shrinks from it,
Fears the white glint of it and cowers away.

WOMAN.

O bid him turn and bid him eat his words
At sight of those who come to bear out mine—
Captains and warrior women! .. Look on her

Photograph by Miss Leon, 30, Regent Street, S.W.   Copyright.

Vera Coburn as the Maid of Saragossa.

Photograph by Miss Leon, 30, Regent Street, S.W.   *Copyright.*

Cicely Hamilton as Christian Davies.

(The Warriors *enter*.)

JOAN OF ARC Brave saint, pure soldier, lily of God and France,
Whose soul fled hence on wings of pain, of fire!
BOADICEA Oh, look on her who stood, a Briton in arms,
And spat defiance at the hosts of Rome!
BLACK AGNES See there, the black-browed Agnes of Dunbar
Who held her fortress as a soldier should
And capped the cannon's roaring with a jest—
MAID OF SARAGOSSA Fit comrade for the girl who, when the guns
Thundered at Saragossa, took her stand
Upon the walls and fired her countrymen
With her own burning courage—or for her,
EMILIA PLATER Emilia Plater, Poland's heroine,
Leader and patriot, dauntless in despair!
Thou dark-eyed princess of an eastern land,
RANEE OF JHANSI Ruler of Jhansi, captain proved in war
Though but a child in years, thou tak'st thy rank
Among thy fellows... These, and many more,
Have nobly fought where need there was to fight—
Have nobly died where need there was to die—
All these, and many more, some named, some nameless,
Have risked their lives as blithely as a man.
And, come to that, we've rough-and-tumbled it!
CHRISTIAN DAVIES Where's Christian Davies, Chelsea pensioner,

Photograph by Miss Leon, 30, Regent Street, S.W.   Copyright.

Christopher St. John as Hannah Snell.

     Who shouldered musket for a dozen fights?
HANNAH
SNELL Where's Hannah Snell, stout private of the line?
MARY ANNE And little Talbot, drummer of King George?
TALBOT And see, she comes, our Lady of the Lamp!
FLORENCE No soldier she, yet not unused to war
NIGHTINGALE Nor fearful of its horrors—death and wounds
     And pestilence—well hast thou fought them, well,
     O Lady on whose shadow kisses fell!

JUSTICE.

There falls a silence.

WOMAN.

        Goddess, he is dumb!

JUSTICE.

Dost thou not speak?

WOMAN.

        Goddess, he slinks away!

(PREJUDICE *goes out.*)

JUSTICE.

Is it e'en so?

WOMAN.

        Yea, I have silenced him:
O give me judgment, give it!

Photograph by Miss Leon, 30, Regent, W. *Copyright.*

Lina Rathbone as Mary Ann Talbot.

Photograph by "Daily Mirror." *Copyright.*

Marion Terry as Florence Nightingale.

JUSTICE.

I give thee judgment—and I judge thee worthy
To attain thy freedom: but 'tis thou alone
Canst show that thou art worthy to retain it.
O Woman with thy feet on an untried path,
O Woman with thine eyes on the dawn of the world,
Thou hast very much to learn.

WOMAN.

     But I shall learn it!

JUSTICE.

Yea, truly; but with suffering.

 (THE WOMAN *kneels before her silent.*)

         Go forth
To achieve with tears; and bear within thy heart
This word of mine—That soul alone is free
Who sees around it never a soul enslaved.
Go forth: the world is thine... Oh, use it well!
Thou hast an equal, not a master, now.

WOMAN
(*rising*).

I have an equal, not a master, now.
I will go speak with him as peer with peer,
Free woman with free man.

Photograph by "Daily Mirror." *Copyright.*

Pauline Chase as Joan of Arc. **Elizabeth Kirby as Boadicea.** **Munci Capel as Ranee of Jhansi.** **Frances Wetherall as Agnes of Dunbar.**

JUSTICE.

      Then let thy words
Be just and wise.

WOMAN.

       They shall be wise and just;
Free words, and therefore honest... Thus I'll speak
 him!
I have no quarrel with you; but I stand
For the clear right to hold my life my own:
The clear, clean right! To mould it as I will,
Not as you will, with or apart from you.
To make of it a thing of brain and blood,
Of tangible substance and of turbulent thought—
No thin, grey shadow of the life of man!
Your love, perchance, may set a crown on it;
But I may crown myself in other ways—
(As you have done who are one flesh with me)
I have no quarrel with you; but, henceforth,
This you must know: The world is mine, as yours,
The pulsing strength and passion and heart of it:
The work I set my hand to, woman's work,
Because I set my hand to it. Henceforth
For my own deeds myself am answerable
To my own soul.

                   For this in days to come
You, too, shall thank me.   Now you laugh, but I
Laugh too, a laughter without bitterness;
Feeling the riot and rush of crowding hopes,
Dreams, longings and vehement powers; and
   knowing this—
'Tis good to be alive when morning dawns!

LEARNED WOMEN

Hypatia.—Born at Alexandria about 370 A.D. Neoplatonist philosopher. Lectured in her native city, thereby incurring the enmity of the Christians, who feared her great influence. Murdered by a mob of her enemies 415 A.D.

St. Teresa.—1515-1582. Spanish saint, writer and reformer. The only woman upon whom the title of Doctor of the Church has ever been conferred.

Lady Jane Grey.—1537-1554. A pupil of Roger Ascham. "Versed in the Greek, Latin, Italian and French languages and had some acquaintance with Hebrew and Arabic." Nominal queen of England for ten days; deposed and executed at the age of seventeen.

Anna Louisa de Stael-Holstein.—1766-1817. Author and politician. Principal works: "Corinne,"

"De l'Allemagne," "Considerations sur la Revolution Française."

Manon Roland.—1756-93. One of the leading intellects of the French Revolution. Shared the fall of the Girondists and died on the scaffold.

Madelène de Scudéry.—1607-1701. Author of "The Grand Cyrus" and other romances. The first person to receive the "Prix d'Eloquence" from the Académie Française.

Jane Austen.—1775-1817. Author of "Sense and Sensibility," "Pride and Prejudice," "Emma," "Mansfield Park," "Northanger Abbey," "Persuasion."

George Sand (Amantine Aurore Dudevant).—1804-76. Author of "Consuelo," "La Comtesse de Rudolstadt," "Mauprat," "Horace," and numerous other novels; also plays.

Caroline Herschell.—1750-1848. Astronomer. Discovered five new comets.

Marie Curie (born Sklodowska).—One of the foremost of living scientists. The discoverer of radium and polonium. Born 1867.

ARTISTS

Sappho.—Born in Lesbos about 630 B.C.; died about 570 B.C. Poet; styled by Plato "the tenth muse."

Vittoria Colonna.—1490-1547. Poet and friend of Michael Angelo.

Maria Angelica Kauffmann.—1742-1807. Painter and engraver. One of the original members of the Royal Academy.

Marie Louise Elizabeth Vigée Lebrun.—1755-1842. Portrait painter and litterateur.

Rosa Bonheur.—1822-99. The famous painter of animals.

Margaret Van Eyck.—Flemish painter. Flourished about 1430.

Marie Anne Cuppi Camargo.—1710-70. A famous opera dancer.

Nance Oldfield.—1683-1730. One of the earliest and most celebrated of English actresses. Played at Drury Lane and the Haymarket theatres.

SAINTS

St. Hilda.—614-80. Founder of Whitby Abbey and Abbess of Hartlepool and Whitby.

Elizabeth Fry.—1780-1845. Philanthropist. Founder of the Association for the Improvement of the Female Prisoners in Newgate. Effected great reforms in prison conditions. A member of the Society of Friends.

St. Elizabeth of Hungary.—1207-31. Daughter of the King of Hungary, wife of the Landgrave of Thuringia. Renowned for her piety and wonderful charity.

St. Catherine of Siena.—1347-80. Saint and politician. Sent by the Tuscan people on an embassy to the Pope to procure removal of ban of excommunication. Helped to bring about the return of the Pope from Avignon to Rome.

HEROINES

Charlotte Corday (Marie Anne Charlotte de Corday d'Armand).—1768-93. The self-appointed executioner of Marat. Died on the scaffold.

Flora Macdonald.—1720-90. The guide and saviour of Prince Charles Edward after his defeat at Culloden.

Kate Barlass.—The name given to Catherine Douglas, who thrust her arm into the staples of a bolt in a vain endeavour to save James I. of Scotland from his murderers (1437).

Grace Darling.—1815-42. Was instrumental in saving the crew of the "Forfarshire," wrecked on the Farne Islands in 1838.

QUEENS

Elizabeth.—1553-1603. Queen of England, 1558.

Victoria.—1819-1901. Queen of Great Britain, 1837.

Zenobia.—Queen of Palmyra from 267 A.D. to 273 A.D. A courageous and accomplished woman; defeated by the Emperor Aurelian, she was carried captive to Rome.

Philippa of Hainault.—1314-69. Wife of Edward III. of England. Froissart gives her credit for organising the army which defeated the Scots at Nevile's Cross during her husband's absence from England. Remembered for her intercession in favour of the burghers of Calais.

Deborah.—" The children of Israel came up to her for judgment."

Isabella of Spain.—1450-1504. Queen of Castile in her own right, joint ruler of Spain with her husband; one of the wisest of Spanish sovereigns. The patron of Columbus.

WARRIORS.

Joan of Arc.—1410-31.   The deliverer of France from the English.   Burnt at Rouen.

Boadicea.—Queen of the Iceni.   Led the British forces against the Romans under Suetonius Paulinus and took poison rather than survive defeat (A.D. 61).

Black Agnes.—1312-69.   Countess of March.   Defended the castle of Dunbar against the English, 1338.

Maid of Saragossa.—The name bestowed upon Agostina, a young girl who distinguished herself at Saragossa when the town was besieged by the French, 1808-9.

Emilia Plater.—1806-31.   A Polish heroine who took a prominent part in the struggle of her country to throw off the yoke of Russia.

Ranee of Jhansi.—1838-58.   Killed fighting against the British in the Indian mutiny.   Said to have been "the best man on the other side."

Christian Davies.—1667-1739. Enlisted as Christopher Welsh. Fought at Blenheim, wounded at Ramillies, pensioned 1712.

Hannah Snell.—1723-92. Served both in the army and navy; wounded at Pondicherry; out-pensioner of Chelsea Hospital, 1750.

Mary Ann Talbot.—1778-1804. Served in Flanders as a drummer boy, 1793; wounded and pensioned.

Florence Nightingale.—Born 1820. The organiser of hospital nursing in the Crimea; the first woman to be decorated with the Order of Merit.

GARDEN CITY PRESS LIMITED, LETCHWORTH

GARDEN CITY PRESS LIMITED, LETCHWORTH

Lightning Source UK Ltd.
Milton Keynes UK
UKOW012129031012

200043UK00004B/64/P